Your Body
Blood

Anna Sandeman

W
FRANKLIN WATTS
LONDON • SYDNEY

New edition published in 2002
© Aladdin Books Ltd 2002
Designed and produced by
Aladdin Books Ltd
28 Percy Street
London W1T 2BZ

*First published in
Great Britain in 2002 by*
Franklin Watts
96 Leonard Street
London EC2A 4XD

Original edition published by
Franklin Watts in 1996

Design: David West Children's Book Design
Designer: Edward Simkins
Editor: Liz White
Illustrator: Ian Thompson
Picture Research: Brooks Krikler Research
Consultants: Dr R Levene MB.BS, DCH, DRCOG
Jan Bastoncino Dip. Ed., teacher of biology and
science to 5-12 year-olds

ISBN 0-7496-4823-6

Printed in U.A.E.

A CIP catalogue record for this book is available from
the British Library.

Photocredits: Abbreviations: t-top, m-middle,
b-bottom, r-right, l-left
All the pictures are by Roger Vlitos apart from the
following pages; 19 & 27 - Science Photo Library; 22-23, 26
& 29br - Frank Spooner Pictures; 28-29 - Spectrum; 28b -
Mary Evans Picture Library

Contents

How much blood?

Ouch! You have cut yourself. Blood oozes out of the wound and trickles down your finger. It is bright red. It feels warm and slightly sticky.

If you cut yourself, the cut should be cleaned and covered up to stop germs from getting in. If the cut is small it will quickly heal.

If the cut is very deep then you may need stitches to hold the cut together until it can heal.

VIRTUALLY
FAT FREE
MILK
HIGH IN CALCIUM

BRITISH PASTEURISED
SKIMMED MILK

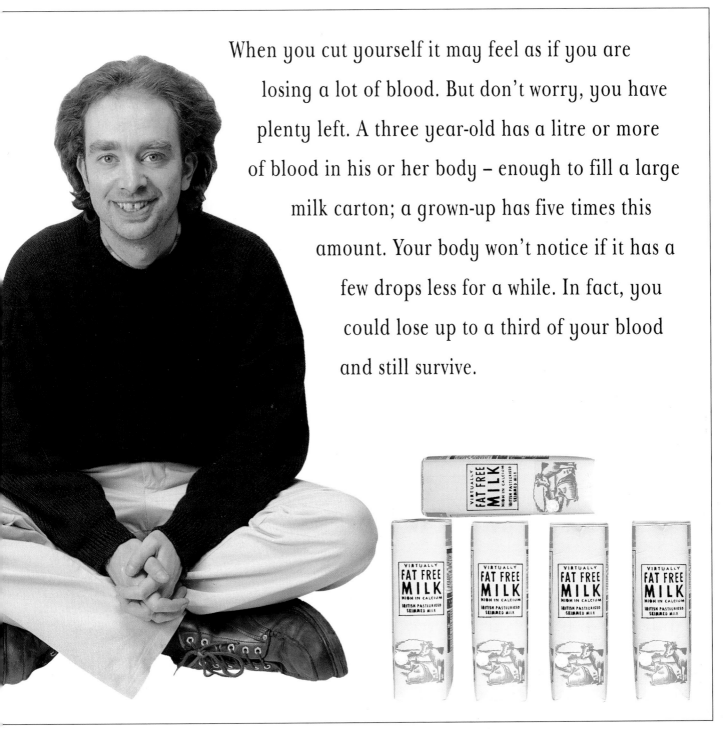

When you cut yourself it may feel as if you are losing a lot of blood. But don't worry, you have plenty left. A three year-old has a litre or more of blood in his or her body – enough to fill a large milk carton; a grown-up has five times this amount. Your body won't notice if it has a few drops less for a while. In fact, you could lose up to a third of your blood and still survive.

What blood does

Your blood travels around your body like a fast-flowing river. The blood flowing through your body is known as your bloodstream. It carries the supplies your body needs to grow and to stay healthy.

Blood also takes away waste and helps your body to fight off disease and to heal wounds.

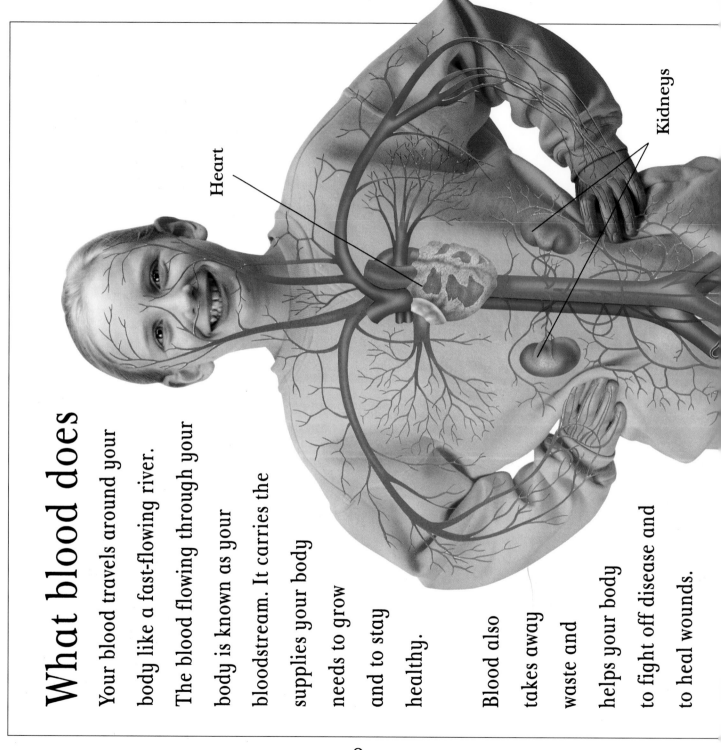

Heart

Kidneys

Most of your blood is made up of a yellowish liquid called plasma. It takes the goodness from the food you eat to all parts of your body.

Plasma also takes waste to your kidneys. Your kidneys then sieve your blood to take out any rubbish. You get rid of the rubbish when you go to the lavatory.

The cleaned blood goes back into your bloodstream to continue its journey round your body.

Blood is pumped around your body by the heart. It travels through veins (shown here in blue) and arteries (shown here in red).

Red cell

White cell

Blood cells

Floating in the plasma are lots of red cells and white cells. You have many more red cells than white cells. It is your red cells which give your blood its colour.

In your lungs red cells take oxygen from the air you breathe in and carry it to all parts of your body. As the red cells give up their oxygen, they collect a gas called carbon dioxide which they take back to your lungs to be breathed out.

In the lungs, blood swaps carbon dioxide for oxygen.

Windpipe

Oxygen

Lung

Carbon dioxide

White cells are much bigger than
red cells. Their job is to kill any
germs which get into your body.

Some germs are so strong they can kill white
cells. If your body is attacked by lots of germs, it makes extra
white cells to fight them off.

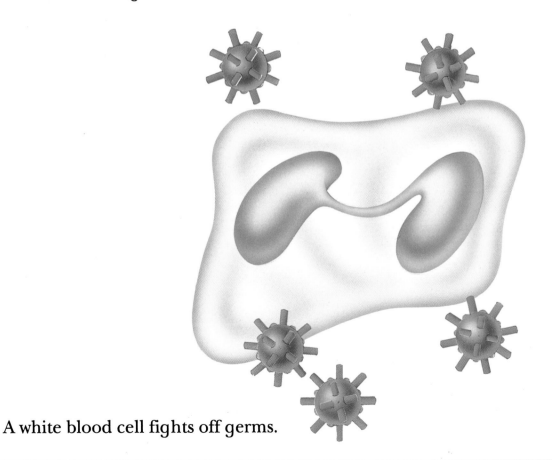

A white blood cell fights off germs.

Cuts and bruises

When you cut yourself, blood flows out quickly at first. But unless the cut is very deep, it soon stops.

Special repair cells in your blood make a kind of glue, which sticks together tiny bits of blood to form a clot.

The clot acts like a plug to stop any more blood from leaking out. It also stops any germs getting in. The clot then dries into a scab, which falls off once new skin has grown underneath.

When did you last get a bruise?
How did it happen?

If you bump yourself
hard you get a bruise.
A bruise is formed
because the blood leaks
into your skin and
makes a blue-black
mark on the surface.
After a few days the
bruise turns yellow. The
leaked blood is gradually
broken down in the skin
and the bruise
fades away.

The working heart

Your blood is pumped around your body by your heart. Without a heart, your blood would quickly sink into your legs and feet! Your heart began pumping long before you were born. It will go on, day and night, throughout your life.

Your heart is about the size of your fist. Stand straight and place your fingers flat against your chest. Slide them slowly up and down until you feel a throbbing. This is your heart pumping.

Now put your ear against a friend's chest. Listen to the heartbeat. You should be able to hear two sounds for each beat.

Squeeze a ball as hard as you can in one hand. You need strong muscles to do it. Your heart is made of strong muscle. Every time your heart beats it squeezes with enough force to pump your blood out and into your arteries.

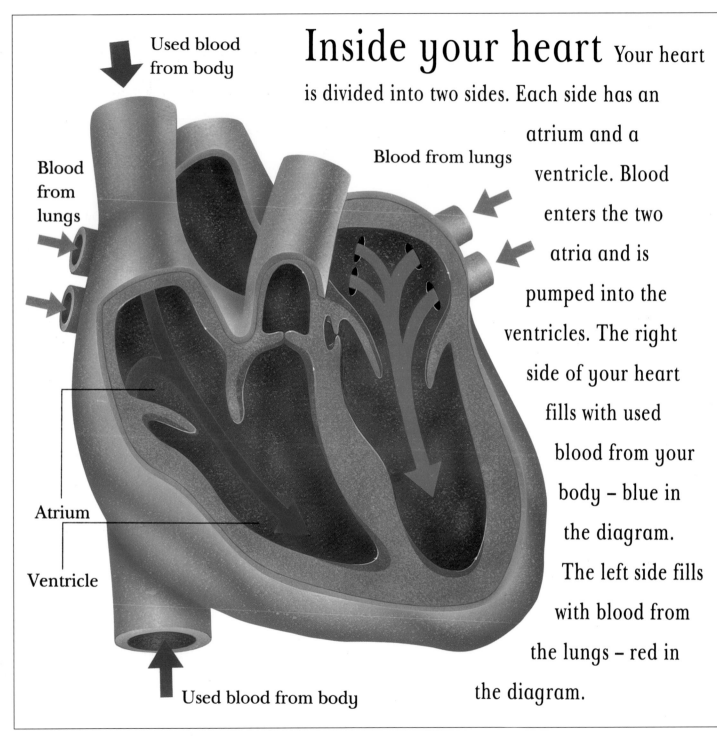

Used blood
from body

Inside your heart
Your heart
is divided into two sides. Each side has an
atrium and a
ventricle. Blood
enters the two
atria and is
pumped into the
ventricles. The right
side of your heart
fills with used
blood from your
body – blue in
the diagram.
The left side fills
with blood from
the lungs – red in
the diagram.

Blood from lungs

Blood
from
lungs

Atrium

Ventricle

Used blood from body

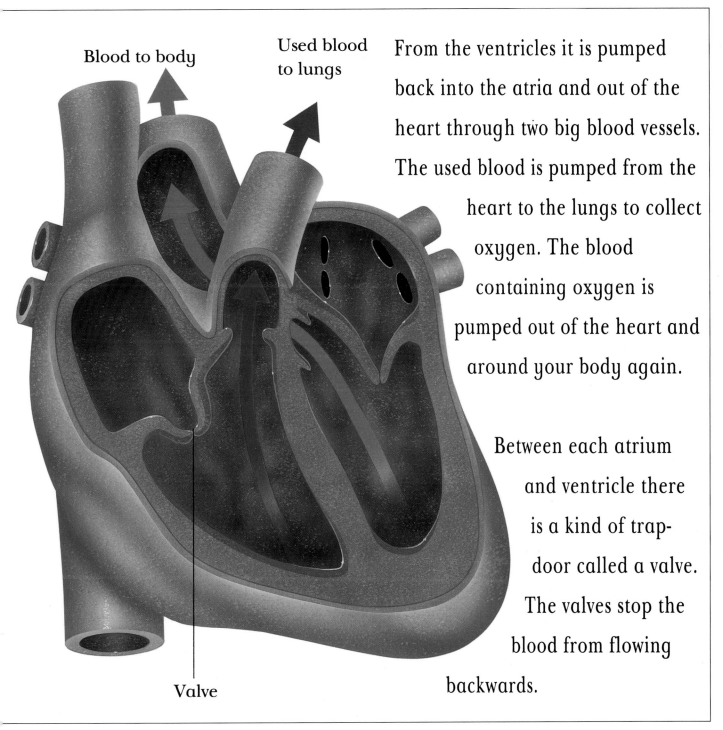

Blood to body

Used blood to lungs

Valve

From the ventricles it is pumped back into the atria and out of the heart through two big blood vessels. The used blood is pumped from the heart to the lungs to collect oxygen. The blood containing oxygen is pumped out of the heart and around your body again.

Between each atrium and ventricle there is a kind of trap-door called a valve. The valves stop the blood from flowing backwards.

Heart

Aorta

Blood vessels
Your blood travels around your body through a network of tubes called blood vessels. The tubes which carry blood away from the heart are called arteries. Those which carry blood back to the heart are called veins. Your aorta is the largest artery in your body. It has thick, elastic walls to squirt blood along your smaller arteries.

Aorta

Artery

Red cell

Thick, elastic walls

White cell

Artery

Your arteries split into smaller and smaller tubes to reach every part of your body. The smallest tubes are called capillaries. These are just wide enough for one red blood cell to pass through at a time. Look closely at your eye. The red threads you can see are capillaries.

Have you noticed that your face often goes red after you have run a race or played an energetic game? Do you know why this happens?

When you are very hot, your capillaries widen so that more blood can reach the surface of your skin to cool down.

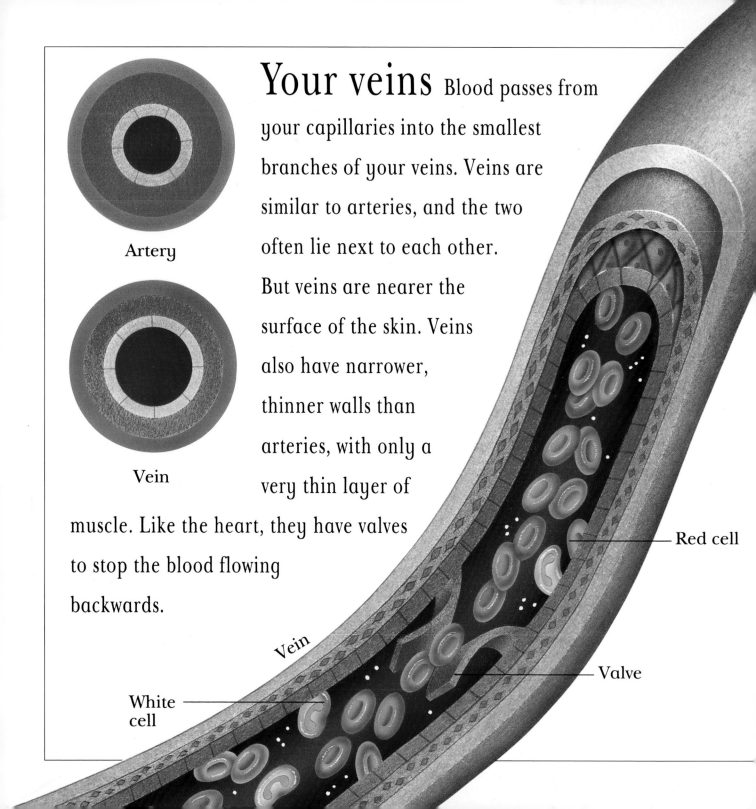

Your veins

Blood passes from your capillaries into the smallest branches of your veins. Veins are similar to arteries, and the two often lie next to each other. But veins are nearer the surface of the skin. Veins also have narrower, thinner walls than arteries, with only a very thin layer of muscle. Like the heart, they have valves to stop the blood flowing backwards.

Artery

Vein

Vein

Red cell

Valve

White cell

The blood in your veins has less oxygen in it than the blood in your arteries. This makes it a dull purply red. Gently bend your hand back and look at your wrist. See how blue your veins seem.

Normally three-fifths of your blood is in your veins. It travels at around 20 centimetres a second. That's about the distance from your wrist to your elbow. In your main arteries, it rushes along at around 32 centimetres a second.

Your pulse

Every time your heart beats, blood is pushed through your arteries. The blood makes your arteries throb. The speed of the throbs is called your pulse rate. An easy place to feel your pulse is at your wrist. Simply rest the fingertips of one hand just below the thumb of your other hand. How many beats can you feel in one minute?

A grown-up's heart beats about 70 times a minute. A child's heart beats faster. Normally the bigger an animal is, the slower its heartbeat. Compare these ...

Mouse - 600 times a minute

Canary - 1,000 times a minute

Human baby - 130 times a minute

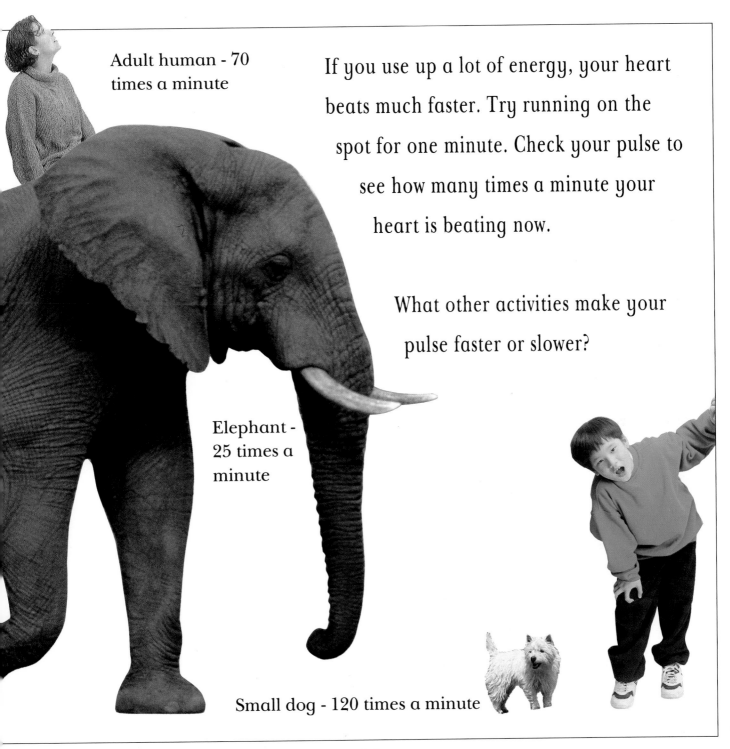

Adult human - 70 times a minute

If you use up a lot of energy, your heart beats much faster. Try running on the spot for one minute. Check your pulse to see how many times a minute your heart is beating now.

What other activities make your pulse faster or slower?

Elephant - 25 times a minute

Small dog - 120 times a minute

Your heart rate

The number of times your heart beats in one minute is called your heart rate. If you use up a lot of energy, your brain sends a message to your heart, telling it to pump more blood to your muscles. Your heart rate speeds up, and so does your pulse.

If your muscles need it, they can demand over four-fifths of your blood. Usually, they work well on only one fifth.

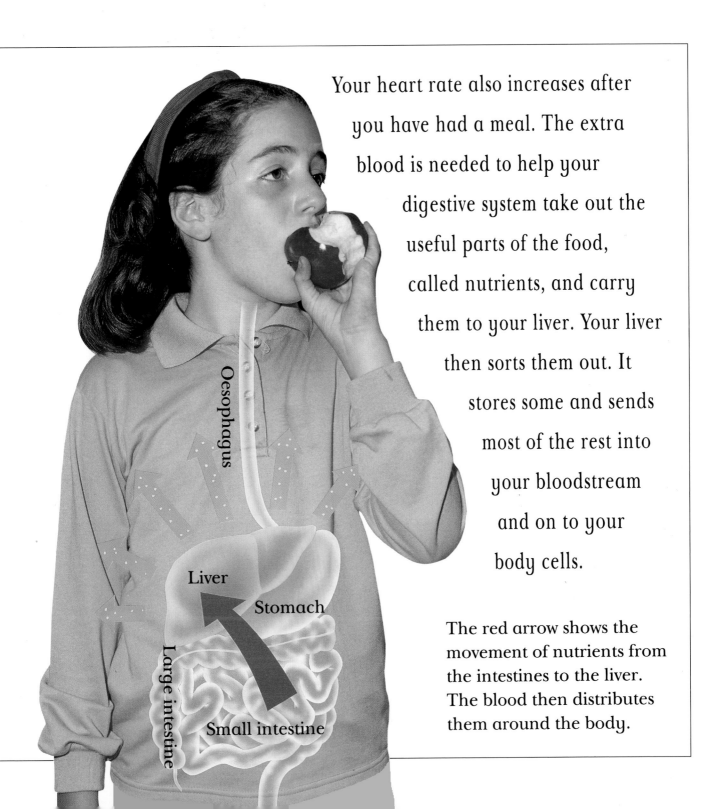

Your heart rate also increases after you have had a meal. The extra blood is needed to help your digestive system take out the useful parts of the food, called nutrients, and carry them to your liver. Your liver then sorts them out. It stores some and sends most of the rest into your bloodstream and on to your body cells.

The red arrow shows the movement of nutrients from the intestines to the liver. The blood then distributes them around the body.

Oesophagus

Liver

Stomach

Large intestine

Small intestine

Blood groups

Not everyone's blood is exactly the same. There are four main blood groups - A, B, AB and O. In some countries, one blood group is much more common than another. Just under half of all the people in the world belong to blood group O.

If someone needs extra blood after an accident or during an operation, doctors have to make sure they give the patient blood which suits their blood group. Someone with blood group A, for example, should not receive group B blood.

Blood is given to hospitals by blood donors. Any healthy grown-up can donate blood. A nurse pricks a vein and draws out up to half a litre of blood. The donor usually notices nothing except the small prick from the needle, and perhaps a little dizziness. The blood is put into a bag and stored in a hospital fridge until it is needed.

Did you know?

... that your heart pumps over four and a half litres (half a bucketful) of blood a minute round your body? That's about 6,500 litres a day.

... that if you could join up all the capillaries in your body they would encircle the world two and a half times?

... that some insects have green blood? Lobsters have blue blood.

... that doctors once used leeches to suck their patients' blood? It was thought to drain sickness from the body.

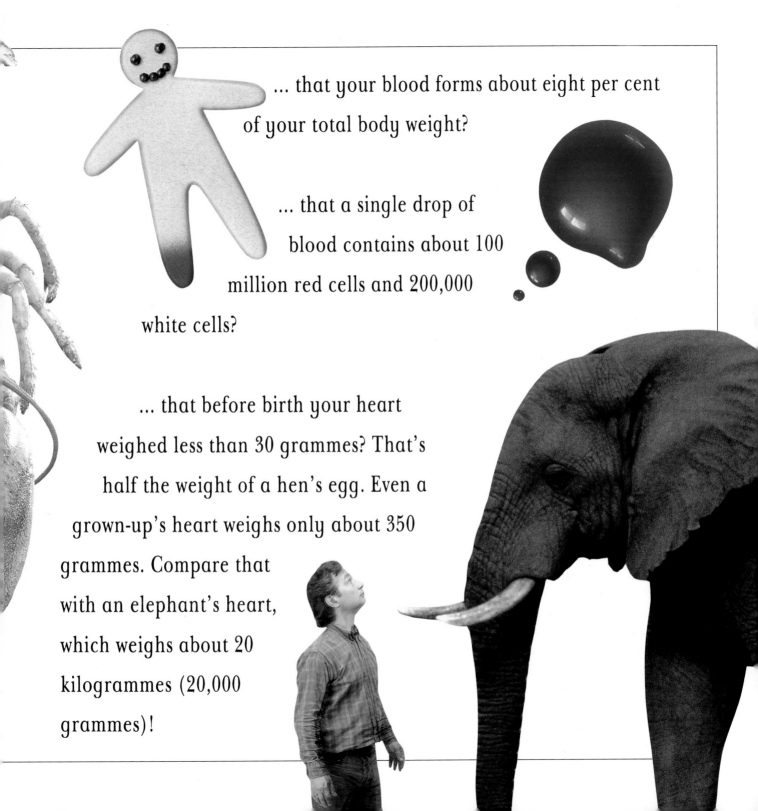

... that your blood forms about eight per cent of your total body weight?

... that a single drop of blood contains about 100 million red cells and 200,000 white cells?

... that before birth your heart weighed less than 30 grammes? That's half the weight of a hen's egg. Even a grown-up's heart weighs only about 350 grammes. Compare that with an elephant's heart, which weighs about 20 kilogrammes (20,000 grammes)!

Glossary

Aorta – The largest artery in your body

Artery – A vessel that carries blood from the heart around the body

Heart – The organ that pumps your blood around your body

Bloodstream – The blood flowing through your body in blood vessels

Plasma – The liquid part of blood

Pulse – The beating of the heart and the arteries that you can feel

Vein – A vessel that carries blood back to your heart from the body

Index

aorta 18, 30

arteries 15, 18, 19, 20,
  21, 22, 30

atrium 16, 17

blood groups 26

bloodstream 8, 9, 13,
  25, 30

blood vessels 18

bruise 13

capillaries 19, 20, 28

carbon dioxide 10

clot 12

germs 11, 12

kidneys 9

liver 25

oxygen 10, 21

plasma 9, 10, 30

pulse 22, 23, 24, 30

valve 17, 20

veins 18, 20, 21, 27, 30

ventricle 16, 17

wound 6, 8

Interested in getting more information on blood and your body?

Check out one of these websites:

www.kidshealth.org

http://www.fi.edu/biosci/heart.html